croche HIP HATS

Beat the summer heat with a selection of chic chapeaux! These caps and hats are easy to crochet and fun to wear, and they'll look great with everything from sundresses to blue jeans. The Big Scoop is an adorable newsboy cap. And Winner's Circle is a stylish jockey cap that will put you ahead of the crowd. Enjoy a day at the beach while wearing First Mate, an updated version of the fisherman's hat. Or treat yourself to the sweetly mingled colors of Ice Cream Social. If you add a scarf and a brooch to your Garden Party hat, you'll be ready for any event of the season. Enjoy your days in the sun with all seven designs. You'll love knowing that you created each one with a crochet hook and ordinary yarn!

LEISURE ARTS, INC.
Little Rock, Arkansas

1. GARDEN PARTY

Shown on page 11.

◼◼◻◻ **EASY**

Finished Size: Adult

MATERIALS

• Medium/Worsted Weight Yarn
  [5 ounces, 236 yards
  (140 grams, 212 meters) per ball]:
  Color A - 2 balls
• Bulky Weight Ribbon Yarn
  [1³/₄ ounces, 115 yards
  (50 grams, 105 meters) per ball]:
  Color B - 3 balls
• Crochet hook, size H (5 mm) **or** size needed
  for gauge
• Scarf and brooch

Entire Hat is worked holding one strand of
Color A and Color B together throughout.

GAUGE SWATCH: 2¹/₂" (6.25 cm)
Work same as Crown through Rnd 4.

CROWN

Holding one strand of Color A and Color B
together, ch 4; join with slip st to form a ring.

Rnd 1 (Right side)**:** Ch 1, 10 sc in ring; join with
slip st to first sc.

Rnd 2: Ch 1, 2 sc in same st and in each sc around;
join with slip st to first sc: 20 sc.

Rnd 3: Ch 1, sc in same st and in each sc around;
join with slip st to first sc.

Rnd 4: Ch 1, sc in same st, 2 sc in next sc, (sc in
next sc, 2 sc in next sc) around; join with slip st to
first sc: 30 sc.

Rnd 5: Ch 1, sc in same st and in each sc around;
join with slip st to first sc.

Rnd 6: Ch 1, sc in same st and in next sc, 2 sc in
next sc, (sc in next 2 sc, 2 sc in next sc) around;
join with slip st to first sc: 40 sc.

Rnd 7: Ch 1, sc in same st and in each sc around;
join with slip st to first sc.

Rnd 8: Ch 1, sc in same st and in next 2 sc, 2 sc in
next sc, (sc in next 3 sc, 2 sc in next sc) around;
join with slip st to first sc: 50 sc.

Rnd 9: Ch 1, sc in same st and in each sc around;
join with slip st to first sc.

Rnd 10: Ch 1, sc in same st and in next 3 sc, 2 sc in next sc, (sc in next 4 sc, 2 sc in next sc) around; join with slip st to first sc: 60 sc.

Rnd 11: Ch 1, sc in same st and in each sc around; join with slip st to first sc.

Rnd 12: Ch 1, sc in same st and in next 4 sc, 2 sc in next sc, (sc in next 5 sc, 2 sc in next sc) around; join with slip st to first sc: 70 sc.

Rnd 13: Ch 1, sc in same st and in each sc around; join with slip st to first sc.

Rnd 14: Ch 1, sc in same st and in next 5 sc, 2 sc in next sc, (sc in next 6 sc, 2 sc in next sc) around; join with slip st to first sc: 80 sc.

Rnd 15: Ch 1, sc in same st and in each sc around; join with slip st to first sc.

Rnd 16: Ch 1, sc in Back Loop Only of same st and each sc around (*Fig. 1, page 21*); join with slip st to **both** loops of first sc.

Rnds 17-27: Ch 1, sc in both loops of same st and each sc around; join with slip st to first sc, do **not** finish off.

BRIM

Rnd 1: Ch 2 **(counts as first hdc, now and throughout)**, hdc in next 6 sc, 2 hdc in next sc, (hdc in next 7 sc, 2 hdc in next sc; join with slip st to first hdc: 90 hdc.

Rnd 2: Ch 1, sc in same st and in each hdc around; join with slip st to first sc.

Rnd 3: Ch 2, hdc in next 7 sc, 2 hdc in next sc, (hdc in next 8 sc, 2 hdc in next sc) around; join with slip st to first hdc: 100 hdc.

Rnd 4: Ch 1, sc in same st and in each hdc around; join with slip st to first sc.

Rnd 5: Ch 2, hdc in next 8 sc, 2 hdc in next sc, (hdc in next 9 sc, 2 hdc in next sc) around; join with slip st to first hdc: 110 hdc.

Rnd 6: Ch 1, sc in same st and in each hdc around; join with slip st to first sc.

Rnd 7: Ch 2, hdc in next 9 sc, 2 hdc in next sc, (hdc in next 10 sc, 2 hdc in next sc) around; join with slip st to first hdc: 120 hdc.

Rnds 8 and 9: Ch 1, sc in same st and in each st around; join with slip st to first sc.

Rnd 10: Ch 2, hdc in next 10 sc, 2 hdc in next sc, (hdc in next 11 sc, 2 hdc in next sc) around; join with slip st to first hdc: 130 hdc.

Rnds 11 and 12: Ch 1, sc in same st and in each st around; join with slip st to first sc.

Rnd 13: Ch 1, sc in same st and in next 11 sc, 2 sc in next sc, (sc in next 12 sc, 2 sc in next sc) around; join with slip st to first sc: 140 sc.

Rnds 14 and 15: Ch 1, sc in same st and in each sc around; join with slip st to first sc.

Rnd 16: Ch 1, **turn**; slip st in each sc around; join with slip st to first slip st, finish off.

2.

FIRST MATE

Shown on page 12.

■■□□ EASY

Finished Size: Adult

MATERIALS

• Medium/Worsted Weight Yarn
  [5 ounces, 236 yards
  (140 grams, 212 meters) per ball]:
  1 ball
• Crochet hook, size F (3.75 mm) **or** size needed
  for gauge

GAUGE SWATCH: 2¹/₂" (6.25 cm)
Work same as Crown through Rnd 4.

STITCH GUIDE

PUFF STITCH (uses one st)
Ch 2, ★ YO, insert hook in st indicated, YO and
pull up a loop; repeat from ★ 3 times **more**,
YO and draw through all 9 loops on hook.

CROWN

Ch 4; join with slip st to form a ring.

Rnd 1 (Right side)**:** Ch 3 **(counts as first dc, now
and throughout)**, 11 dc in ring; join with slip st to
first dc: 12 dc.

Rnd 2: Ch 1, 2 sc in same st and in each dc around;
join with slip st to first sc: 24 sc.

Rnd 3: Ch 1, sc in same st and in each sc around;
join with slip st to first sc.

Rnd 4: Ch 1, sc in same st, 2 sc in next sc, (sc in
next sc, 2 sc in next sc) around; join with slip st to
first sc: 36 sc.

Rnd 5: Ch 1, sc in same st and in each sc around;
join with slip st to first sc.

Rnd 6: Ch 3, dc in next sc, 2 dc in next sc, (dc in
next 2 sc, 2 dc in next sc) around; join with slip st to
first dc: 48 dc.

Rnd 7: Ch 1, sc in same st and in each dc around;
join with slip st to first sc.

Rnd 8: Ch 1, sc in same st and in next 2 sc, 2 sc in
next sc, (sc in next 3 sc, 2 sc in next sc) around; join
with slip st to first sc: 60 sc.

Rnd 9: Work Puff St in same st, ch 1, skip next sc,
★ work Puff St in next sc, ch 1, skip next sc; repeat
from ★ around; join with slip st to first
Puff St: 30 Puff Sts and 30 chs.

Rnd 10: Ch 1, sc in same st and in each st around;
join with slip st to first sc: 60 sc.

Rnd 11: Ch 2 **(counts as first hdc)**, hdc in next 3 sc, 2 hdc in next sc, (hdc in next 4 sc, 2 hdc in next sc) around; join with slip st to first hdc: 72 hdc.

Rnd 12: Ch 1, sc in same st and in next 4 hdc, 2 sc in next hdc, (sc in next 5 hdc, 2 sc in next hdc) around; join with slip st to first sc: 84 sc.

Rnd 13: Work Puff St in same st, ch 1, skip next sc, ★ work Puff St in next sc, ch 1, skip next sc; repeat from ★ around; join with slip st to first Puff St: 42 Puff Sts and 42 chs.

Rnd 14: Ch 1, sc in same st and in each st around; join with slip st to first sc: 84 sc.

Rnd 15: Ch 1, sc in same st, ch 1, skip next sc, (sc in next sc, ch 1, skip next sc) around; join with slip st to first sc: 42 sc and 42 ch-1 sps.

Rnds 16-19: Ch 1, (sc in next ch-1 sp, ch 1) around; join with slip st to first sc.

Rnd 20: Ch 1, sc in same st and in each st around; join with slip st to first sc: 84 sc.

Rnd 21: Work Puff St in same st, ch 1, skip next sc, ★ work Puff St in next sc, ch 1, skip next sc; repeat from ★ around; join with slip st to first Puff St: 42 Puff Sts and 42 chs.

Rnd 22: Ch 1, sc in same st and in each st around; join with slip st to first sc, do **not** finish ff: 84 sc.

BRIM

Rnd 1: Ch 2 **(counts as first hdc)**, hdc in next 5 sc, 2 hdc in next sc, (hdc in next 6 sc, 2 hdc in next sc) around; join with slip st to first hdc: 96 hdc.

Rnd 2: Ch 1, sc in same st and in each hdc around; join with slip st to first sc.

Rnd 3: Ch 1, sc in same st and in next 6 sc, 2 sc in next sc, (sc in next 7 sc, 2 sc in next sc) around; join with slip st to first sc: 108 sc.

Rnd 4: Ch 1, sc in same st and in each sc around; join with slip st to first sc.

Rnd 5: Ch 1, sc in same st and in next 7 sc, 2 sc in next sc, (sc in next 8 sc, 2 sc in next sc) around; join with slip st to first sc: 120 sc.

Rnd 6: Ch 1, sc in same st and in each sc around; join with slip st to first sc.

Rnd 7: Ch 1, sc in same st and in next 8 sc, 2 sc in next sc, (sc in next 9 sc, 2 sc in next sc) around; join with slip st to first sc: 132 sc.

Rnd 8: Ch 1, sc in same st and in each sc around; join with slip st to first sc.

Rnd 9: Ch 1, sc in same st and in next 9 sc, 2 sc in next sc, (sc in next 10 sc, 2 sc in next sc) around; join with slip st to first sc: 144 sc.

Rnds 10-12: Ch 1, sc in same st and in each sc around; join with slip st to first sc.

Rnd 13: Ch 1, **turn**; slip st in each sc around; join with slip st to first slip st, finish off.

THE BIG SCOOP

Shown on Front Cover.

Finished Size: Adult

MATERIALS

- Medium/Worsted Weight Yarn
  [6 ounces, 330 yards
  (170 grams, 301 meters) per skein]: 1 skein
- Crochet hook, size I (5.5 mm) **or** size needed
  for gauge

Entire Hat is worked holding two strands of
yarn together throughout.

GAUGE SWATCH: 2¹/₂" (6.25 cm)
Work same as Crown through Rnd 3.

STITCH GUIDE

DECREASE (uses next 2 sc)
YO, pull up a loop in next 2 sc, YO and draw
through all 4 loops on hook **(counts as one
hdc)**.

CROWN

Holding two strands of yarn together, ch 4;
join with slip st to form a ring.

Rnd 1 (Right side)**:** Ch 1, 12 sc in ring; join with
slip st to first sc.

Note: Loop a short piece of yarn around any sc to
mark Rnd 1 as **right** side.

Rnd 2: Ch 2 **(counts as first hdc, now and
throughout)**, hdc in same st, 2 hdc in next sc and
in each sc around; join with slip st to first hdc:
24 hdc.

Rnd 3: Ch 1, sc in same st and in each hdc around;
join with slip st to first sc.

Rnd 4: Ch 2, 2 hdc in next sc, (hdc in next sc,
2 hdc in next sc) around; join with slip st to first
hdc: 36 hdc.

Rnd 5: Ch 1, sc in same st and in each hdc around;
join with slip st to first sc.

Rnd 6: Ch 2, hdc in next sc, 2 hdc in next sc,
(hdc in next 2 sc, 2 hdc in next sc) around; join with
slip st to first hdc: 48 hdc.

Rnd 7: Ch 1, sc in same st and in each hdc around;
join with slip st to first sc.

Rnd 8: Ch 2, hdc in next 2 sc, 2 hdc in next sc,
(hdc in next 3 sc, 2 hdc in next sc) around; join with
slip st to first hdc: 60 hdc.

Rnd 9: Ch 1, sc in same st and in each hdc around;
join with slip st to first sc.

Rnd 10: Ch 2, hdc in next 3 sc, 2 hdc in next sc,
(hdc in next 4 sc, 2 hdc in next sc) around; join with
slip st to first hdc: 72 hdc.

Rnd 11: Ch 1, sc in same st and in each hdc around; join with slip st to first sc.

Rnd 12: Ch 2, hdc in next 4 sc, 2 hdc in next sc, (hdc in next 5 sc, 2 hdc in next sc) around; join with slip st to first hdc: 84 hdc.

Rnd 13: Ch 1, sc in same st and in each hdc around; join with slip st to first sc.

Rnd 14: Ch 2, hdc in next sc and in each sc around; join with slip st to first hdc.

Rnd 15: Ch 1, sc in same st and in each hdc around; join with slip st to first sc.

Rnds 16-19: Repeat Rnds 14 and 15 twice.

Rnd 20: Ch 2, hdc in next 4 sc, decrease, (hdc in next 5 sc, decrease) around; join with slip st to first hdc: 72 hdc.

Rnd 21: Ch 1, sc in same st and in each hdc around; join with slip st to first sc.

Rnd 22: Ch 2, hdc in next 3 sc, decrease, (hdc in next 4 sc, decrease) around; join with slip st to first hdc: 60 hdc.

Rnd 23: Ch 1, sc in same st and in each hdc around; join with slip st to first sc.

Rnd 24: Ch 1, sc in Front Loop Only of same st and each sc around *(Fig. 1, page 21)*; join with slip st to **both** loops of first sc.

Rnd 25: Ch 1, sc in both loops of same st and each sc around; join with slip st to first sc, finish off.

BILL
TOP
Row 1: Working in Front Loops Only, skip first 13 sc from joining and join yarn with sc in next sc *(see Joining With Sc, page 20)*; sc in next 3 sc, 2 sc in next sc, (sc in next 5 sc, 2 sc in next sc) twice, sc in next 4 sc, leave remaining sc unworked: 24 sc.

Row 2: Ch 1, turn; skip first sc, slip st in next sc, sc in next 4 sc, hdc in next 3 sc, dc in next 6 sc, hdc in next 3 sc, sc in next 4 sc, skip next sc, slip st in last sc: 22 sts.

Row 3: Ch 1, turn; skip first slip st, slip st in next sc, sc in next sc, 2 sc in next sc, hdc in next sc, 2 hdc in next hdc, (dc in next st, 2 dc in next st) twice, dc in next 2 dc, (2 dc in next st, dc in next st) twice, 2 hdc in next hdc, hdc in next sc, 2 sc in next sc, sc in next sc, slip st across to Row 1; do **not** finish off.

BOTTOM
Row 1: Ch 1, turn; working in free loops of sc on Rnd 25 of Crown in front of Top *(Fig. 2a, page 21)*, sc in next 4 sc, 2 sc in next sc, (sc in next 5 sc, 2 sc in next sc) twice, sc in next 3 sc: 24 sc.

Rows 2 and 3: Work same as Top.

JOINING
Ch 1, turn; working through **both** thicknesses on Top and Bottom, sc in end of each row and in each st across; finish off.

4. BRIMMING WITH FUN

Shown on page 13.

◼◼◻◻ **EASY**

Finished Size: Adult

MATERIALS

- Medium/Worsted Weight Yarn
  [5 ounces, 236 yards
  (140 grams, 212 meters) per ball]:
  Color A - 1 ball
- Super Bulky Weight Ribbon Yarn
  [1¾ ounces, 110 yards
  (50 grams, 100 meters) per ball]:
  Color B - 3 balls
- Crochet hook, size I (5.5 mm) **or** size needed
  for gauge

Entire Hat is worked holding one strand of
Color A and Color B together throughout.

GAUGE SWATCH: 2¾" (7 cm)
Work same as Crown through Rnd 2.

CROWN

Holding one strand of Color A and Color B
together, ch 4; join with slip st to form a ring.

Rnd 1 (Right side)**:** Ch 3 **(counts as first dc, now
and throughout)**, 11 dc in ring; join with slip st to
first dc: 12 dc.

Rnd 2: Ch 3, dc in same st, 2 dc in next dc and in
each dc around; join with slip st to first dc: 24 dc.

Rnd 3: Ch 3, 2 dc in next dc, (dc in next dc, 2 dc in
next dc) around; join with slip st to first dc: 36 dc.

Rnd 4: Ch 3, dc in next dc, 2 dc in next dc, (dc in
next 2 dc, 2 dc in next dc) around; join with slip st
to first dc: 48 dc.

Rnd 5: Ch 3, dc in next 2 dc, 2 dc in next dc, (dc in
next 3 dc, 2 dc in next dc) around; join with slip st
to first dc: 60 dc.

Rnd 6: Ch 2 **(counts as first hdc, now and
throughout)**, hdc in next 8 dc, 2 hdc in next dc,
(hdc in next 9 dc, 2 hdc in next dc) around; join
with slip st to first hdc: 66 hdc.

Rnd 7: Ch 1, sc in Back Loop Only of same st and
each hdc around *(Fig. 1, page 21)*; join with slip st
to **both** loops of first sc.

Rnd 8: Ch 2, hdc in both loops of next sc and each
sc around; join with slip st to first hdc.

Rnd 9: Ch 1, sc in same st and in each hdc around;
join with slip st to first sc.

Rnds 10-15: Repeat Rows 8 and 9, 3 times.

Rnd 16: Ch 2, hdc in next 9 sc, 2 hdc in next sc, (hdc in next 10 sc, 2 hdc in next sc) around; join with slip st to first hdc: 72 hdc.

Rnd 17: Ch 1, sc in same st and in each hdc around; join with slip st to first sc, do **not** finish off.

BRIM

Rnd 1: Ch 1, sc in same st and in next 4 sc, 2 sc in next sc, (sc in next 5 sc, 2 sc in next sc) around; join with slip st to first sc: 84 sc.

Rnds 2 and 3: Ch 1, sc in same st and in each sc around; join with slip st to first sc.

Rnd 4: Ch 1, sc in same st and in next 5 sc, 2 sc in next sc, (sc in next 6 sc, 2 sc in next sc) around; join with slip st to first sc: 96 sc.

Rnds 5-11: Ch 1, sc in same st and in each sc around; join with slip st to first sc.

Rnd 12: Ch 1, sc in same st and in next 14 sc, 2 sc in next sc, (sc in next 15 sc, 2 sc in next sc) around; join with slip st to first sc: 102 sc.

Rnd 13: Ch 1, sc in same st and in each sc around; join with slip st to first sc.

Rnd 14: Ch 1, **turn**; slip st in each sc around; join with slip st to first slip st, finish off.

5. WINNER'S CIRCLE

Shown on page 14.

◼️◼️◻️◻️ EASY

Finished Size: Adult

MATERIALS

• Medium/Worsted Weight Yarn [7 ounces, 364 yards (198 grams, 333 meters) per skein]: 1 skein
• Crochet hook, size J (6 mm) **or** size needed for gauge

Entire Hat is worked holding two strands of yarn together throughout.

GAUGE SWATCH: 3¼" (8.25 cm)
Work same as Crown through Rnd 2, page 10.

Instructions begin on page 10.

CROWN

Holding two strands of yarn together, ch 4; join with slip st to form a ring.

Rnd 1 (Right side)**:** Ch 3 **(counts as first dc, now and throughout)**, 11 dc in ring; join with slip st to first dc: 12 dc.

Rnd 2: Ch 3, dc in same st, 2 dc in next dc and in each dc around; join with slip st to first dc: 24 dc.

Rnd 3: Ch 3, 2 dc in next dc, (dc in next dc, 2 dc in next dc) around; join with slip st to first dc: 36 dc.

Rnd 4: Ch 3, dc in next dc, 2 dc in next dc, (dc in next 2 dc, 2 dc in next dc) around; join with slip st to first dc: 48 dc.

Rnds 5-9: Ch 3, dc in next dc and in each dc around; join with slip st to first dc, do **not** finish off.

BILL
TOP

Row 1: Ch 1, working in Front Loops Only *(Fig. 1, page 21)*, sc in next 3 dc, hdc in next 3 dc, dc in next 12 dc, hdc in next 3 dc, sc in next 3 dc, slip st in next dc, leave remaining 22 dc unworked: 26 sts.

Row 2: Ch 1, turn; working in both loops, skip first slip st, slip st in next sc, sc in next 3 sts, hdc in next 3 sts, dc in next dc, 2 dc in next dc, (dc in next 2 dc, 2 dc in next dc) twice, dc in next dc, hdc in next 3 sts, sc in next 3 sts, slip st in last 2 sc: 27 sts.

Row 3: Ch 1, turn; skip first slip st, slip st in next 2 sts, sc in next 3 sts, hdc in next 2 hdc, 2 dc in next dc, (dc in next dc, 2 dc in next dc) twice, dc in next 2 dc, 2 dc in next dc, (dc in next dc, 2 dc in next dc) twice, hdc in next 2 hdc, sc in next 3 sts, slip st in last 2 sts: 32 sts.

Row 4: Ch 1, turn; skip first slip st, slip st in next 2 sts, sc in next 3 sts, hdc in next 3 sts, (dc in next dc, 2 dc in next dc) twice, dc in next 2 dc, 2 dc in each of next 2 dc, dc in next 2 dc, (2 dc in next dc, dc in next dc) twice, hdc in next 3 sts, sc in next 3 sts, slip st in next 2 sts, leave last slip st unworked: 36 sts.

Row 5: Ch 1, turn; skip first slip st, slip st in next 2 sts, sc in next 3 sts, hdc in next 4 sts, dc in next 16 dc, hdc in next 4 sts, sc in next 3 sts, slip st across to Row 1; do **not** finish off.

BOTTOM

Row 1: Ch 1, turn; working in free loops of dc on Rnd 9 of Crown in front of Top *(Fig. 2a, page 21)*, sc in next 3 dc, hdc in next 3 dc, dc in next 12 dc, hdc in next 3 dc, sc in next 3 dc, slip st in next dc: 26 sts.

Rows 2-5: Work same as Top.

JOINING AND EDGING

Ch 1, turn; working through **both** thicknesses on Top and Bottom, sc in end of each row and in each st across, sc in each dc on Rnd 9; join with slip st to first sc, finish off.

(1)

11

6

14

ICE CREAM SOCIAL

Shown on Back Cover.

Finished Size: Adult

■■□□ **EASY**

MATERIALS

- Medium/Worsted Weight Yarn
  [5 ounces, 278 yards (141 grams,
  254 meters) per skein]: 1 skein

  MEDIUM 4

- Crochet hook, size I (5.5 mm) **or** size needed
  for gauge

Entire Hat is worked holding two strands of
yarn together throughout.

GAUGE SWATCH: 3¼" (8.25 cm)
Work same as Crown through Rnd 2.

STITCH GUIDE

PICOT
Ch 4, slip st in fourth ch from hook.

CROWN

Holding two strands of yarn together, ch 4; join
with slip st to form a ring.

Rnd 1 (Right side)**:** Ch 3 **(counts as first dc, now
and throughout)**, 11 dc in ring; join with slip st to
first dc: 12 dc.

Rnd 2: Ch 3, dc in same st, 2 dc in next dc and in
each dc around; join with slip st to first dc: 24 dc.

Rnd 3: Ch 3, 2 dc in next dc, (dc in next dc, 2 dc in
next dc) around; join with slip st to first dc: 36 dc.

Rnd 4: Ch 3, dc in next dc, 2 dc in next dc, (dc in
next 2 dc, 2 dc in next dc) around; join with slip st
to first dc: 48 dc.

Rnds 5-9: Ch 3, dc in next dc and in each dc
around; join with slip st to first dc, do **not** finish off.

BRIM

Rnd 1: Ch 1, working in Back Loops Only *(Fig. 1,
page 21)*, sc in same st and in next 3 dc, work
Picot, (sc in next 4 dc, work Picot) around; join with
slip st to Back Loop Only of first sc: 12 Picots.

Rnd 2: Ch 2 **(counts as first hdc)**, working behind
Picots and in Back Loops Only, hdc in next 2 sc,
2 hdc in next sc, (hdc in next 3 sc, 2 hdc in next sc)
around; join with slip st to first hdc: 60 hdc.

Rnd 3: Ch 1, sc in both loops of same st and each
hdc around; join with slip st to first sc.

Rnd 4: Ch 3, dc in next 3 sc, 2 dc in next sc,
(dc in next 4 sc, 2 dc in next sc) around; join with
slip st to first dc: 72 dc.

Rnd 5: Ch 3, dc in next 4 dc, 2 dc in next dc,
(dc in next 5 dc, 2 dc in next dc) around; join with
slip st to first dc: 84 dc.

Rnd 6: Ch 3, dc in next 5 dc, 2 dc in next dc,
(dc in next 6 dc, 2 dc in next dc) around; join with
slip st to first dc, finish off.

7. SPECIAL INTEREST

Shown on page 15.

■■□□ EASY

Finished Size: Adult

MATERIALS

• Medium/Worsted Weight Yarn
 [2¹/₂ ounces, 120 yards (70 grams,
 109 meters) per ball for solid **or** 2 ounces,
 95 yards (56 grams, 86 meters) per ball for
 Variegated]:
 Variegated - 3 balls
 Blue - 1 ball
• Crochet hook, size F (3.75 mm) **or** size needed
 for gauge
• Yarn needle

GAUGE SWATCH: 2¹/₄" (5.5 cm)
Work same as Crown through Rnd 2.

STITCH GUIDE

BEGINNING CLUSTER (uses one st)
Ch 2, ★ YO, insert hook in st indicated, YO and
pull up a loop, YO and draw through 2 loops
on hook; repeat from ★ once **more**, YO and
draw through all 3 loops on hook.
CLUSTER (uses one st)
★ YO, insert hook in st indicated, YO and pull
up a loop, YO and draw through 2 loops on
hook; repeat from ★ 2 times **more**, YO and
draw through all 4 loops on hook.

TREBLE CROCHET (abbreviated tr)
YO twice, insert hook in st indicated, YO and
pull up a loop (4 loops on hook), (YO and draw
through 2 loops on hook) 3 times.
JOINING DOUBLE TREBLE CROCHET
 (abbreviated joining dtr)
YO 3 times, insert hook in last ch, YO and pull
up a loop (5 loops on hook), YO and draw
through 2 loops on hook, skip next sc on
Rnd 3, insert hook in next sc, YO and draw
through st **and** next 2 loops on hook, (YO and
draw through 2 loops on hook) twice.

CROWN

With Variegated, ch 4; join with slip st to form a
ring.

Rnd 1 (Right side)**:** Ch 3 **(counts as first dc, now
and throughout)**, 11 dc in ring; join with slip st to
first dc: 12 dc.

Rnd 2: Ch 1, 2 sc in same st and in each dc
around; join with slip st to first sc: 24 sc.

Rnd 3: Ch 1, sc in same st and in each sc around;
join with slip st to first sc.

Rnd 4: Ch 2 **(counts as first hdc, now and
throughout)**, 2 hdc in next sc, (hdc in next sc,
2 hdc in next sc) around; join with slip st to
first hdc: 36 hdc.

Instructions continued on page 18.

Rnd 5: Ch 1, sc in same st and in each hdc around; join with slip st to first sc.

Rnd 6: Ch 3, dc in next sc, 2 dc in next sc, (dc in next 2 sc, 2 dc in next sc) around; join with slip st to first dc: 48 dc.

Rnd 7: Ch 1, sc in same st and in each dc around; join with slip st to first sc.

Rnd 8: Ch 1, sc in same st and in next 2 sc, 2 sc in next sc, (sc in next 3 sc, 2 sc in next sc) around; join with slip st to first sc: 60 sc.

Rnd 9: Work Beginning Cluster in same st, ch 1, skip next sc, ★ work Cluster in next sc, ch 1, skip next sc; repeat from ★ around; join with slip st to top of Beginning Cluster: 30 Clusters and 30 chs.

Rnd 10: Ch 1, sc in same st and in each st around; join with slip st to first sc: 60 sc.

Rnd 11: Ch 2, hdc in next 3 sc, 2 hdc in next sc, (hdc in next 4 sc, 2 hdc in next sc) around; join with slip st to first hdc: 72 hdc.

Rnd 12: Ch 1, sc in same st and in each hdc around; join with slip st to first sc.

Rnd 13: Ch 1, sc in same st and in next 4 sc, 2 sc in next sc, (sc in next 5 sc, 2 sc in next sc) around; join with slip st to first sc: 84 sc.

Rnd 14: Work Beginning Cluster in same st, ch 1, skip next sc, ★ work Cluster in next sc, ch 1, skip next sc; repeat from ★ around; join with slip st to top of Beginning Cluster: 42 Clusters and 42 chs.

Rnd 15: Ch 1, sc in same st and in each st around; join with slip st to first sc: 84 sc.

Rnd 16: Ch 2, hdc in next sc and in each sc around; join with slip st to first hdc.

Rnd 17: Ch 1, sc in same st and in each hdc around; join with slip st to first sc.

Rnd 18: Work Beginning Cluster in same st, ch 1, skip next sc, ★ work Cluster in next sc, ch 1, skip next sc; repeat from ★ around; join with slip st to top of Beginning Cluster: 42 Clusters and 42 chs.

Rnds 19 and 20: Ch 1, sc in same st and in each st around; join with slip st to first sc: 84 sc.

Rnd 21: Ch 3, dc in next sc and in each sc around; join with slip st to first dc.

Rnd 22: Ch 1, sc in same st and in each dc around; join with slip st to first sc, do **not** finish off.

BRIM

Rnd 1: Ch 2, hdc in next 5 sc, 2 hdc in next sc, (hdc in next 6 sc, 2 hdc in next sc) around; join with slip st to first hdc: 96 hdc.

Rnd 2: Ch 1, sc in same st and in each hdc around; join with slip st to first sc.

Rnd 3: Ch 2, hdc in next 6 sc, 2 hdc in next sc, (hdc in next 7 sc, 2 hdc in next sc) around; join with slip st to first hdc: 108 hdc.

Rnd 4: Ch 1, sc in same st and in each hdc around; join with slip st to first sc.

Rnd 5: Ch 1, sc in same st and in next 7 sc, 2 sc in next sc, (sc in next 8 sc, 2 sc in next sc) around; join with slip st to first sc: 120 sc.

Rnds 6 and 7: Ch 1, sc in same st and in each sc around; join with slip st to first sc.

Rnd 8: Ch 1, sc in same st and in next 8 sc, 2 sc in next sc, (sc in next 9 sc, 2 sc in next sc) around; join with slip st to first sc: 132 sc.

Rnds 9 and 10: Ch 1, sc in same st and in each sc around; join with slip st to first sc.

Rnd 11: Ch 1, sc in same st and in next 9 sc, 2 sc in next sc, (sc in next 10 sc, 2 sc in next sc) around; join with slip st to first sc: 144 sc.

Rnds 12 and 13: Ch 1, sc in same st and in each sc around; join with slip st to first sc.

Rnd 14: Ch 1, **turn**; slip st in each sc around; join with slip st to first slip st, finish off.

STAR

With Blue, ch 4; join with slip st to form a ring.

Rnd 1: Ch 1, 10 sc in ring; join with slip st to first sc.

Rnd 2: Ch 1, 2 sc in same st and in each sc around; join with slip st to first sc: 20 sc.

Rnd 3: Ch 1, sc in same st and in each sc around; join with slip st to first sc.

Rnd 4: Ch 1, sc in same st, ★ † ch 6, sc in second ch from hook, hdc in next ch, dc in next ch, tr in next ch, work joining dtr **(point made)**, skip next sc †, sc in next sc; repeat from ★ 3 times **more**, then repeat from † to † once; join with slip st to first sc: 5 points.

Rnd 5: Ch 1, working in free loops of chs *(Fig. 2b, page 21)*, sc in same st and in each st around; join with slip st to first sc, finish off.

Sew Star to top of Crown.

HATBAND

With Blue, chain a 30" (76 cm) length. Slip st in second ch from hook and in each ch across; finish off.

Working under 2 dc and over 2 dc, weave Hatband through Rnd 21 on Crown.

GENERAL INSTRUCTIONS

ABBREVIATIONS

ch(s)	chain(s)
cm	centimeters
dc	double crochet(s)
dtr	double treble crochet(s)
hdc	half double crochet(s)
mm	millimeters
Rnd(s)	Round(s)
sc	single crochet(s)
sp(s)	space(s)
st(s)	stitch(es)
tr	treble crochet(s)
YO	yarn over

★ — work instructions following ★ as many **more** times as indicated in addition to the first time.

† to † — work all instructions from first † to second † **as many** times as specified.

( ) or [ ] — work enclosed instructions **as many** times as specified by the number immediately following **or** work all enclosed instructions in the stitch or space indicated **or** contains explanatory remarks.

colon (:) — the number(s) given after a colon at the end of a row or round denote(s) the number of stitches or spaces you should have on that row or round.

GAUGE

Exact gauge is **essential** for proper size and fit. Before beginning your project, make the sample swatch given in the individual instructions in the yarn and hook specified. After completing the swatch, measure it, counting your stitches and rows or rounds carefully. If your swatch is larger or smaller than specified, **make another, changing hook size to get the correct gauge**. Keep trying until you find the size hook that will give you the specified gauge.

HINTS

As in all crocheted pieces, good finishing techniques make a big difference in the quality of the piece.

Make a habit of taking care of loose ends as you work. Thread a yarn needle with the yarn end. With **wrong** side facing, weave the needle through several inches, then reverse the direction and weave it back through several inches. When ends are secure, clip them off close to work.

JOINING WITH SC

When instructed to join with sc, begin with a slip knot on hook. Insert hook in stitch or space indicated, YO and pull up a loop, YO and draw through both loops on hook.

BACK OR FRONT LOOP ONLY

Work only in loop(s) indicated by arrow (*Fig. 1*).

Fig. 1

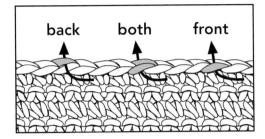

FREE LOOPS

After working in Back or Front Loops Only on a row or round, there will be a ridge of unused loops. These are called the free loops. Later, when instructed to work in the free loops of the same row or round, work in these loops (*Fig. 2a*).

When instructed to work in free loops of a chain, work in loop indicated by arrow (*Fig. 2b*).

Fig. 2a

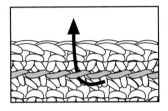

Fig. 2b

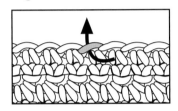

CROCHET TERMINOLOGY	
UNITED STATES	**INTERNATIONAL**
slip stitch (slip st) =	single crochet (sc)
single crochet (sc) =	double crochet (dc)
half double crochet (hdc) =	half treble crochet (htr)
double crochet (dc) =	treble crochet (tr)
treble crochet (tr) =	double treble crochet (dtr)
double treble crochet (dtr) =	triple treble crochet (ttr)
triple treble crochet (tr tr) =	quadruple treble crochet (qtr)
skip =	miss

Yarn Weight Symbol & Names	SUPER FINE 1	FINE 2	LIGHT 3	MEDIUM 4	BULKY 5	SUPER BULKY 6
Type of Yarns in Category	Sock, Fingering Baby	Sport, Baby	DK, Light Worsted	Worsted, Afghan, Aran	Chunky, Craft, Rug	Bulky, Roving
Crochet Gauge Ranges in Single Crochet to 4" (10 cm)	21-32 sts	16-20 sts	12-17 sts	11-14 sts	8-11 sts	5-9 sts
Advised Hook Size Range	B-1 to E-4	E-4 to 7	7 to I-9	I-9 to K-10.5	K-10.5 to M-13	M-13 and larger

ALUMINUM CROCHET HOOKS													
U.S.	B-1	C-2	D-3	E-4	F-5	G-6	H-8	I-9	J-10	K-10½	N	P	Q
Metric - mm	2.25	2.75	3.25	3.5	3.75	4	5	5.5	6	6.5	9	10	15

◼◻◻◻ **BEGINNER**	Projects for first-time crocheters using basic stitches. Minimal shaping.
◼◼◻◻ **EASY**	Projects using yarn with basic stitches, repetitive stitch patterns, simple color changes, and simple shaping and finishing.
◼◼◼◻ **INTERMEDIATE**	Projects using a variety of techniques, such as basic lace patterns or color patterns, mid-level shaping and finishing.
◼◼◼◼ **EXPERIENCED**	Projects with intricate stitch patterns, techniques and dimension, such as non-repeating patterns, multi-color techniques, fine threads, small hooks, detailed shaping and refined finishing.

BASIC STITCHES

CHAIN

To work a chain stitch, begin with a slip knot on the hook. Bring the yarn **over** hook from back to front, catching the yarn with the hook and turning the hook slightly toward you to keep the yarn from slipping off. Draw the yarn through the slip knot *(Fig. 3)* **(first chain stitch made,** *abbreviated ch)*.

Fig. 3

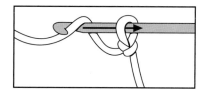

WORKING INTO THE CHAIN

When counting chains, always begin with the first chain from the hook and then count toward the beginning of your foundation chain *(Fig. 4a)*.

Fig. 4a

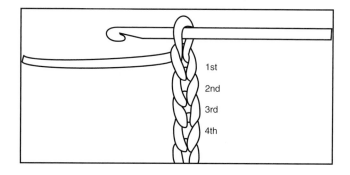

1st
2nd
3rd
4th

Method 1: Insert hook into back ridge of each chain *(Fig. 4b)*.

Fig. 4b

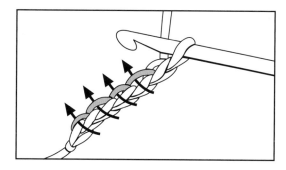

Method 2: Insert hook under top two strands of each chain *(Fig. 4c)*.

Fig. 4c

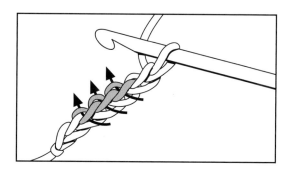

SLIP STITCH

To work a slip stitch, insert hook in stitch or space indicated, YO and draw through stitch and through loop on hook *(Fig. 5)* **(slip stitch made,** *abbreviated slip st)*.

Fig. 5

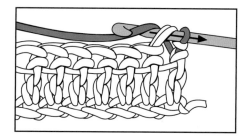

SINGLE CROCHET

Insert hook in stitch or space indicated, YO and pull up a loop, YO and draw through both loops on hook *(Fig. 6)* **(single crochet made,** *abbreviated sc).*

Fig. 6

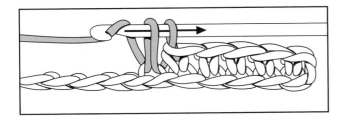

HALF DOUBLE CROCHET

YO, insert hook in stitch or space indicated, YO and pull up a loop, YO and draw through all 3 loops on hook *(Fig. 7)* **(half double crochet made,** *abbreviated hdc).*

Fig. 7

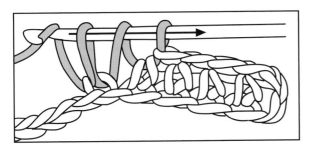

DOUBLE CROCHET

YO, insert hook in stitch or space indicated, YO and pull up a loop (3 loops on hook), YO and draw through 2 loops on hook *(Fig. 8a)*, YO and draw through remaining 2 loops on hook *(Fig. 8b)* **(double crochet made,** *abbreviated dc).*

Fig. 8a

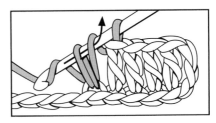

Fig. 8b

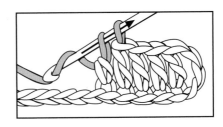

TREBLE CROCHET

YO twice, insert hook in stitch or space indicated, YO and pull up a loop (4 loops on hook) *(Fig. 9a)*, (YO and draw through 2 loops on hook) 3 times *(Fig. 9b)* **(treble crochet made,** *abbreviated tr).*

Fig. 9a

Fig. 9b

23

YARN INFORMATION

Each project in this leaflet was made with Medium/Worsted Weight Yarn, Bulky Weight Yarn, and Super Bulky Weight Yarn. Any brand of the same weight yarn may be used. It is best to refer to the yardage/meters when determining how many balls or skeins to purchase. Remember, to arrive at the finished size, it is the GAUGE/TENSION that is important, not the brand of yarn.

For your convenience, listed below are the specific yarns used to create our photography models.

1. GARDEN PARTY
Lion Brand® Lion Cotton
Color A - #186 Maize
Lion Brand® Trellis
Color B - #303 Champagne

2. FIRST MATE
Lion Brand® Lion Cotton
#100 White

3. THE BIG SCOOP
Caron® Simply Soft®
#9748 Rubine Red
Caron® Simply Soft Brites®
#9610 Grape
#9607 Limelight

4. BRIMMING WITH FUN
Lion Brand® Lion Cotton
Color A - #140 Rose
Lion Brand® Incredible
Color B - #206 Autumn Leaves

5. WINNER'S CIRCLE
Red Heart® Super Saver®
#776 Dk Orchid, #774 Lt Raspberry, and #943 Blueberry Pie

6. ICE CREAM SOCIAL
Red Heart® Super Saver®
#320 Cornmeal, #380 Windsor Blue, and #994 Banana Berry

7. SPECIAL INTEREST
Lily® Sugar 'N Cream®
Variegated - #00178 Potpourri Print
Blue - #00026 Light Blue

Production Team: Technical Editors - Lois J. Long; Editorial Writer - Susan McManus Johnson; Graphic Artist - Steph Johnson; and Photo Stylist - Cassie Francioni.